COPYRIGHT © 2022
BY DENISE 'RENAE' BRACKETT

All Rights Reserved

This book or any portion thereof may not be
reproduced or used in any manner whatsoever
without the express written permission of the
author.

Printed in the United States of America

DEDICATION

This book is dedicated to all the children who love to listen. If you are a great listener, then I bet that you are very obedient as well.
I know you will enjoy and learn more about the ear in this book.

When God made us, He gave our body parts names. Each of those parts has a different role to play in our well-being.

Only the ears hear.

Come, let us find out what only the ears hear.

ONLY THE EARS HEAR...

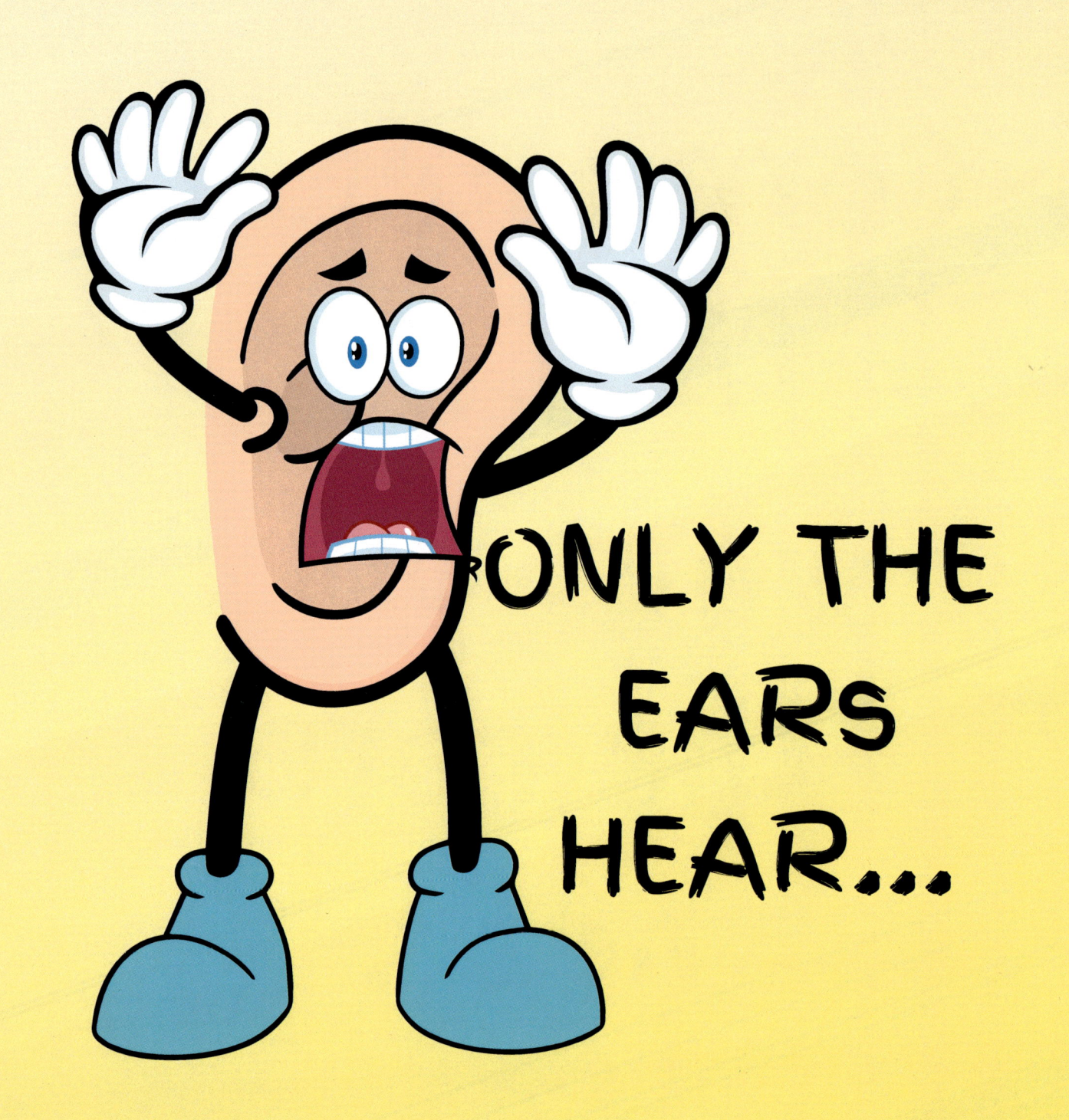

The sound of the school bell as I walk into school.

ONLY THE EARS HEAR...

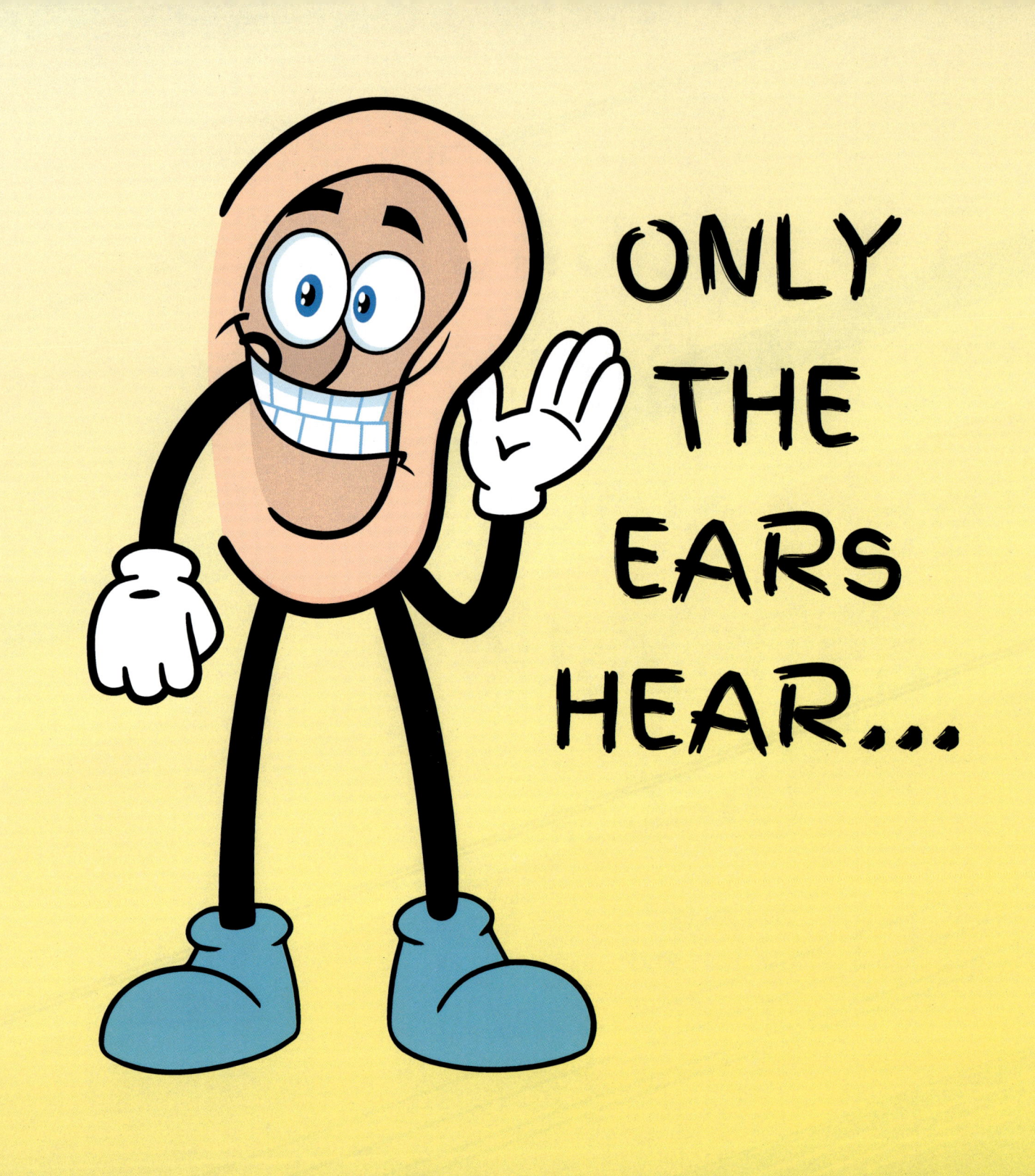

The sound of the fire engine as it rushes by to put out a fire.

ONLY THE EARS HEAR....

The sound of my dog Bingo barking as we play.

ONLY THE EARS HEAR...

The sound of the brush as I get my teeth cleaned at the dentist.

ONLY THE EARS HEAR...

The sound of the water as I take a shower.

ONLY THE EARS HEAR....

The sound of the sound of my baby sister crying.

ONLY THE EARS HEAR...

The sound of my dad snoring in the living room chair.

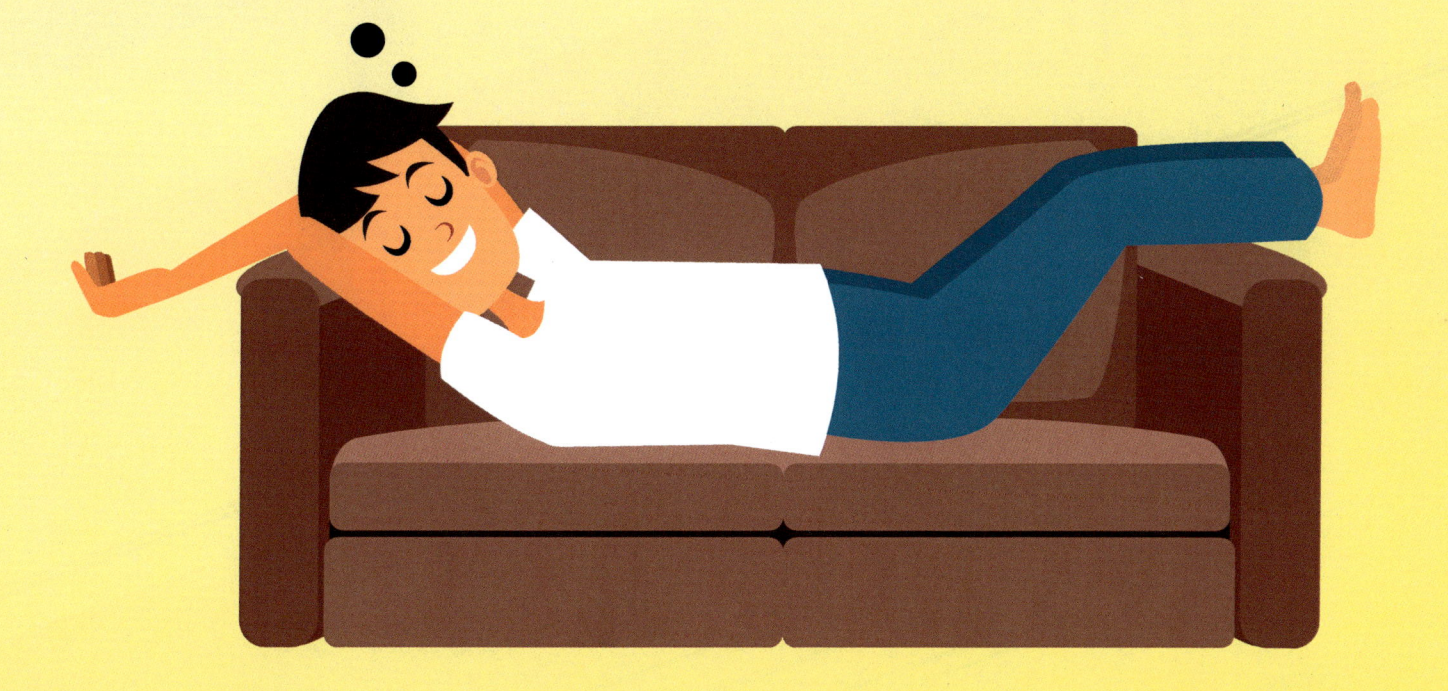

ONLY THE EARS HEAR ...

The sound of the music as we sing and dance.

ONLY THE EARS HEAR...

The sound of my wheelchair as I swoosh by.

ONLY THE EARS HEAR....

When mummy whispers, "I love you".

Shhh... did you hear that?

I bet you didn't, because only the ears can hear it.

THE END!